THE BIG BOOK OF

EMPOWERING AFFIRMATIONS

— FOR —

BLACK KIDS

1000 Positive Affirmations to Nurture Self-Love, Boost Self-Esteem, Build Unshakable Confidence and Inspire Greatness within

SHANICE DANIELS

TABLE OF CONTENTS

INTRODUCTION

I0559310

Are you ready to change your life? I hope so! You are holding a book that can help you do just that.

This book uses stories from Black history to create affirmations that can inspire kids of all races. Black history is full of powerful stories and lessons that can help us every day. From a long time ago, our people have been lifting each other with wise words, sayings, and songs. This book is a collection of those affirmations, inspired by our rich history, with tips on how to use them and even create your own.

This book is divided into three parts. Part One explains what an affirmation is and how to use it. We'll talk about the challenges you might face today and how these affirmations can help you feel more confident and strong.

Part Two is all about the affirmations. You can read it from start to finish or jump around to find the ones that speak to you. Whether you need them now or in the future, these affirmations are here to help. The nine chapters include:

1. Affirmations for Achieving Goals
2. Affirmations for Resilience and Overcoming Failure
3. Affirmations for Self-Esteem
4. Affirmations for Inner Peace/Overcoming Stress
5. Affirmations for Leading
6. Affirmations for Social Interaction
7. Affirmations for Positive Attitude
8. Affirmations for Making the World a Better Place
9. Affirmations for Gratitude
10. Affirmations for Champions

We've numbered the affirmations to make them easy to find, but they're not in any special order. Feel free to explore and find the ones that mean the most to you.

As you grow, you'll learn to be your own coach. Right now, you're working with your parents, teachers, and community members. You'll need to encourage yourself during tough times, stay excited for new challenges, and keep going even when things are good. Affirmations are a powerful tool to help you stay motivated, build self-esteem, and keep moving forward on your amazing journey.

You're becoming a coach, so it's fitting you should have a playbook. Ready to study a playbook, coach? Let's get to it!

PART 1
AN INTRODUCTION TO AFFIRMATIONS

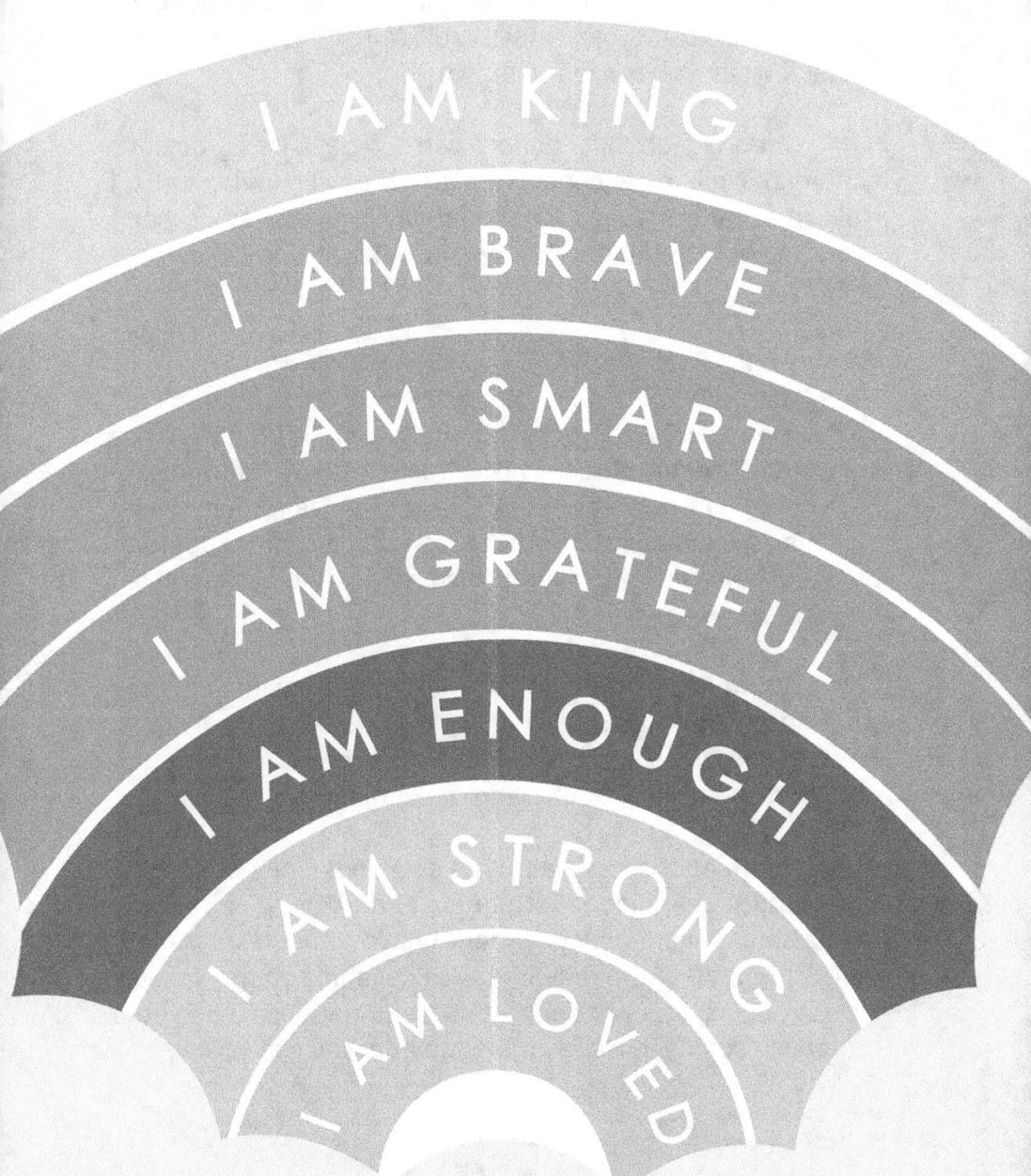

CHAPTER 1:
WHAT ARE AFFIRMATIONS?

Hey, coach! Can I call you coach? Whether you like it or not, you are a life coach, and the life you are coaching is your own. You get to decide the plays. You are responsible for bringing out the best in yourself. You'll have to motivate yourself when you're feeling down.

It's a big job, but I believe you can do it. Using positive statements will make coaching yourself easier. In this book, I will explain affirmations, give you many examples to use, and show you how to create your own affirmations based on your needs.

What is an "Affirmation"?

Don't let the big word intimidate you. "Affirmation" is a big word for a small phrase and a simple idea. An "affirmation" is a short, positive phrase about yourself. "I am proud of who I am" is an example of an affirmation. It's a simple, uplifting phrase. The term "affirmation" also means the act of saying the phrase.

Affirming something means agreeing with it. When you say an affirmation out loud, you are agreeing with it. Affirmations are a type of self-talk where you imagine the person you want to become and make that vision real.

Affirmations can help with struggles; they offer hope and strength. Everyone has struggles, and everyone can benefit from affirmations. I coach myself; I have struggles; I benefit from affirmations. You're going to be coaching yourself; you'll face struggles; you will benefit from affirmations. These little sentences can have a big impact on how you see yourself.

When you feel negative or overwhelmed, remember an affirmation, and those feelings will start to fade. For example, if your teacher gives you ten pages of reading for homework, you might feel overwhelmed. But if you remember the affirmation, "I am good at studying," the assignment becomes more manageable.

WHY USE AFFIRMATIONS?

As you grow up, you won't always have others to support you. You'll need to become your own mentor and recognize your own strengths and abilities. It will be up to you to take care of yourself.

Who is going to motivate you? You are. Who is going to encourage positive changes in your life? You are. Who is going to boost your self-esteem? You are. Who is going to coach you to success? You are! One of the greatest coaching tools you can have is affirmations. What makes them so great? Here are eleven things that affirmations do for us:

- Affirmations can motivate you. Positive affirmations can help you stay motivated by replacing negative thoughts with positive ones.
- Affirmations remind us of our worth and value. They boost your confidence and self-worth.
- Affirmations reduce stress. When we remember that we are capable, we find ways to get things done.
- Affirmations increase happiness. They help you see the positives in difficult situations.
- Affirmations give us confidence. For example, if you tell yourself "I am brave," you might start to feel brave and act brave.
- Affirmations help us bounce back from setbacks. They make us resilient.
- Affirmations guide us. They are like guiding stars for making decisions in life.

- Affirmations have physical and psychological effects. They boost serotonin and reduce cortisol levels.
- Affirmations remind us that we are empowered. They remind us that we have control over our lives and emotions.
- Affirmations celebrate the past, help us thrive in the present, and prepare us for the future. They reflect our heritage and help us plan for the future.

WHY THESE AFFIRMATIONS ARE BASED ON BLACK LIVES

People of all races can benefit from affirmations; struggles like feeling like an outsider or facing discrimination are universal. Unlike other affirmation books, though, the affirmations in this book are based on Black lives of the past for the challenges Black youth encounter today. Those challenges include:

Unfair stereotypes. Blacks are often shown in a bad way in the media. Affirmations can help us see our own value. Struggles with identity. Some Blacks have trouble knowing who they are because they don't see a variety of successful Black people to look up to.

Anxiety about achieving dreams. Black individuals often worry about achieving their goals because they think they might face racism and constant struggle.
Peer pressure. Black people also face pressure from their own community. Affirmations can help you stay strong in the face of peer pressure.

Pride and mental health. Blacks are very proud, but sometimes too proud to admit when they need help. Affirmations remind us that mental health matters.

CHAPTER 2:
HOW TO USE AFFIRMATIONS?

Now is the time to start using positive statements to boost your confidence. Just like you would plan a garden, you need to choose what affirmations to plant in your mind. In Part II of this book, you will find a large assortment of affirmations. Pick and choose the ones you want to incorporate into your life. If you don't like what you see, in Part III, we will talk about how to write your own affirmations.

It's important to keep repeating these affirmations to yourself to make them stick. They may not have an immediate effect, but they will help you during challenging times in the future. So, start now and be ready to use them when life gets tough.

HOW TO USE AFFIRMATIONS

Okay, coach, we've talked about what an affirmation is and why it is important. Now we need to talk about how to use affirmations. Just like a gardener must water and weed the seeds she planted if she expects them to grow, you must nurture your affirmations if you expect them to take root in your mind.

People absorb affirmations in different ways—some by listening, some by reading, some by saying them aloud, and some by actively engaging in a routine. What works for one person may not work for another. It's best to try different methods and see what works best for you. Choose an affirmation that resonates with you. Decide if you'll focus on it for a day or a week. Pick how many times a day you'll remind yourself of the affirmation. There's no correct way to do this— find what works best for you. Here are some common ways:

Use it as a wake-up call. When you go to sleep at night, choose the affirmation for the next day and place it on the nightstand by your bed. When you wake up, say it aloud. Think about what it means for you. Hearing it, seeing it, and pondering it will set the tone for the day. Saying a positive affirmation is a great way to start the day and puts you in a positive mindset for the day ahead.

Say it to the person in the mirror. Stand in front of the mirror and look yourself in the eye. Repeat the affirmation, watching yourself take a stand for this important principle.

Write it. Remember having to write, "I will not talk in class" on the board? You remember exactly what you wrote, don't you? Many people learn best by writing things. Write the affirmation five times or however many times it takes for you to memorize it.

Journal it. Write down the affirmation and then free-write how you can apply it to your life. Freewriting is a stream-of-consciousness exercise; just write whatever comes to mind and see where it takes you.

Visualize it. Having read and said the affirmation, close your eyes and picture how you will behave. For instance, if your affirmation is "I am a good public speaker," picture yourself standing at the front of the class giving your presentation. Visualizing allows you to see the affirmation put into action.

Sing it. Put the affirmation to a tune. Just as many of us learned our ABCs thanks to the ABC Song, we can learn affirmations as well.

Use it as a good night closing. An affirmation is also a great way to end the day. By pondering your affirmation at bedtime, you set a can-do attitude for the next day and relax your mind so sleep comes easier.

Create an affirmation ritual. A ritual is a step-by-step process that you follow each time. This can be as simple as waking up each morning and saying the affirmation aloud, or as complex as reading it silently, reading it aloud, writing it five times, freewriting about it for five minutes, and then saying it aloud again as you close your notebook. The goal is to make the affirmation an unconscious part of your thinking. Once you have found a ritual that works, stick with it; you may not see results immediately, but they will appear in time.

WHAT CAN YOU DO WITH PAST AFFIRMATIONS?

Once an affirmation is used, it has hopefully become a part of your mind, but it likely needs repetition. Here are some ways to keep an affirmation in front of you even after you have moved on to other affirmations:

- Post the affirmation on the refrigerator. Every time you open the refrigerator, you will see the affirmation.
- Place the affirmation on the bathroom mirror. When you brush your teeth or comb your hair, you can refresh your memory by reading the affirmation again.
- Create a poster. Use the affirmation as the basis of a poster.
- Use it as a bookmark. Use a copy of your typed or handwritten affirmation to mark your place in a book.
- Create a collage. A collage can celebrate groups of affirmations. For instance, you might have a "Joy" collage with affirmations related to joy.
- Create a card deck. Write each affirmation on an index card. Pull a card from the deck when you need a reminder.
- Make a screen saver. Place your favorite affirmation on a background and set it as your screensaver.
- Place it on a bulletin board. Whenever you feel down, look at the bulletin board to remind yourself of the affirmation.

- Create a review jar. Place used affirmations in a jar. Pull one out periodically to refresh yourself.
- Share the affirmation with a parent or friend. Get your family and friends to say it with you. Sharing your affirmations helps keep you accountable.

Conclusion

Affirmations can be used in many ways. Find the way(s) that works best for you – and then use them.

PART 2
ALL ABOUT AFFIRMATIONS

STAY AMAZING

CHAPTER 3: AFFIRMATIONS FOR ACHIEVING GOALS

Goals give guidance to our lives, helping us choose a path out of the many possibilities in front of us. Whitney M. Young, Jr., the American civil rights leader, said, "Stretch your mind and fly." One goal you might have is to complete high school, so to reach that goal, you attend school, study, and do homework. Setting goals is great, but turning those goals into success requires a lot of work. Here are some affirmations to keep you focused on your goals:

1. I am ready to work hard to achieve my goals.

2. I love to learn new things and grow my knowledge.

3. I try new things every day to discover what I enjoy.

4. I am excited about what's ahead and ready for new adventures.

5. I am planning for a bright future with goals and dreams.

6. I am growing stronger and smarter every day.

7. I learn something new every day to become a better me.

8. I push myself to do my best in everything I do.

9. I am open to new adventures and experiences.

10. I welcome new ideas that help me think creatively.

11. I embrace challenges and learn from them.

12. I am stretching my mind to learn new things every day.

13. I will shine today by doing my best.

14. I set goals for myself and work hard to achieve them.

15. I am the captain of my life, steering my own course.

16. I believe I can reach my goals with hard work and dedication.

17. I am moving forward in life, step by step.

18. I can handle any challenge that comes my way.

19. I use my mistakes to learn and grow.

20. I am worthy of good things and believe in myself.

21. I do what needs to be done to reach my goals.

22. I learn more about myself each day and what I am capable of.

23. I strive for excellence in everything I do.

24. I am chasing my dreams and making them a reality.

25. I am a winner because I never give up.

26. I am always learning and growing.

27. I am on the right path to success.

28. I am working hard to reach my goals every day.

29. I look for chances to grow and improve.

30. I seek out new opportunities to learn.

31. I take smart risks to achieve my dreams.

32. I practice to get better and better.

33. I am a great student, eager to learn.

34. I am excited about my future and all it holds.

35. I see a bright future for myself and work towards it.

36. I am willing to work hard now for a great future.

37. I can achieve anything I set my mind to if I work hard.

38. I am up for a challenge and ready to take it on.

39. I am curious like a detective, always looking for answers.

40. I am going to shine in everything I do.

41. I will reach my goals with determination.

42. I have a bright future ahead of me.

43. I find joy in working hard and achieving my dreams.

44. I am making my dreams come true step by step.

45. I am making today great with positive actions.

46. I am moving forward with my goals every day.

47. I can create the life I want with effort and focus.

48. I think positively today and every day.

49. I control my goals and work towards them.

50. I control my life and make positive choices.

51. I control my future with my actions today.

52. I am preparing for tomorrow by working hard today.

53. My goals are within reach if I keep working hard.

54. Every expert started as a beginner, just like me.

55. I know where I'm headed and plan my path.

56. I get ready to face challenges with preparation.

57. I am responsible for my life and my choices.

58. I am responsible for my feelings and my reactions.

59. I respect myself and my abilities.

60. I can adapt to new situations and thrive.

61. I am flexible like a gymnast, ready to adjust.

62. I set deadlines I can meet and work towards them.

63. I adjust to changing situations with ease.

64. I am ready for challenges and eager to face them.

65. I am always getting better and improving.

66. I improve every day with practice and effort.

67. I am creative like an artist, finding new ways to express myself.

68. I do my best in every situation, no matter what.

69. I am committed to my goals and work hard for them.

70. My life has direction and purpose.

71. I work hard and it pays off.

72. I am motivated to reach my dreams.

73. I will reach my goals with perseverance.

74. I put effort into my goals every day.

75. I am excited about my future and what I can achieve.

76. I can do what I set my mind to with hard work.

77. I have plans for my future and work towards them.

78. I've got this, no matter what comes my way.

79. I take responsibility for my actions and learn from them.

80. I take responsibility for myself and my growth.

81. I can do hard things and overcome challenges.

82. I plan my work and then work my plan to success.

83. My dreams are worth chasing and I will achieve them.

84. I believe in my abilities and trust myself.

85. I am becoming a better me every day.

86. I am dedicated to improving and growing.

87. I win fair and square by working hard.

88. I share my goals with others to stay accountable.

89. I help others with their goals and support them.

90. I am always growing and learning.

91. I have many talents and I use them well.

92. My goals are achievable and within reach.

93. I am responsible for my dreams and making them real.

94. I am responsible for my goals and work towards them.

95. I discover new things daily that help me improve.

96. I am confident in my abilities and strengths.

97. I know I am a winner, even if I fail sometimes. 98. I am doing my best and proud of my efforts.

99. I am goal-oriented and focused on my dreams.

100. I am proud of my progress and keep moving forward.

CHAPTER 4:
AFFIRMATIONS FOR RESILIENCE AND OVERCOMING FAILURE

Everyone faces setbacks sometimes. What makes successful people different is that they don't let failure stop them. Michael Jordan, a fantastic basketball player, once said, "I can accept failure. Everyone fails at something. But I can't accept not trying." They learn from their mistakes and try again.

Resilience means more than just bouncing back from failure. It means pushing through tough times and being able to adapt to change while still doing well. As the poet Maya Angelou said, "I can be changed by what happens to me. But I refuse to be reduced by it."

Here are some affirmations to help you build resilience and overcome failure:

101. I am asking for help when needed.

102. I will be the best I can be.

103. I will be open to change.

104. I will find a way.

105. I am adaptable.

106. I am flexible.

107. I am resilient.

108. I am willing to try again.

109. I am learning something each day.

110. I will keep moving forward.

111. I find a different way if the first way doesn't work.

112. I am willing to learn.

113. I admit I don't know it all.

114. I am improving each day.

115. I am willing to fail as I push myself to do better.

116. I am a go-getter.

117. I am living life to the fullest.

118. Failing isn't a reason to quit.

119. If I get knocked down, I will get back up.

120. Challenges help me grow stronger.

121. I grow by overcoming challenges.

122. I remember why I chose my goals.

123. I am going to be successful.

124. Failing at something doesn't make me a failure.

125. Failures often come before success.

126. Tests are an opportunity for me to show what I know.

127. I am a problem solver.

128. I keep working on a problem even if it is difficult.

129. Failure is a chance to try a different way.

130. I am better because of the challenges I face.

131. I accept challenges.

132. I am willing to try again if I don't succeed the first time.

133. I am a winner, even if I am losing at a particular moment.

134. I will put in the time required to find a solution to a problem.

135. I am open-minded.

136. I know setbacks are a part of life.

137. I refuse to let fear stop me.

138. I keep up with changes.

139. I can accept new ways of doing old things.

140. I am giving my all to whatever I do.

141. If I can't make it through an obstacle, I will find a way around it.

142. I am willing to do what it takes to reach my goals.

143. I may not be perfect, but I am valuable.

144. I am willing to accept challenges.

145. I will step back and regroup when needed, but I won't give up.

146. I learn from my mistakes.

147. I ask for advice when I need it.

148. Failure is only temporary.

149. I am always growing.

150. I am excited about new opportunities.

151. I am able to work through whatever life gives me.

152. I look for opportunities to grow.

153. I overcome my mistakes.

154. I am able to adjust for setbacks.

155. I have the strength I need to face today.

156. I embrace new ways of doing things.

157. I am able to find good things in every change.

158. I accept responsibility for my mistakes.

159. I am meeting my goals despite challenges.

160. I find the bright side to any failure I have.

161. I enjoy challenges.

162. I can achieve my goals with hard work.

163. I am persistent.

164. I am comfortable taking risks to learn new things.

165. I am determined.

166. I am going after my dreams, even if I have a setback.

167. Despite setbacks, I have confidence in my abilities.

168. My dreams are worth going after, even if they are not easy to achieve.

169. I am worthy of respect, even though I do fail from time to time.

170. I am always learning.

171. I am open to trying new things.

172. I am capable of meeting my goals.

173. I am learning from my setbacks.

174. I am strong, and I can face whatever life throws at me.

175. I am going to keep trying until I succeed.

176. I am able to turn problems into opportunities.

177. I am not defined by my problems; I am defined by how I handle them.

178. I am able to find the positive, even in times of change.

179. I am able to find the positive, even in times of discouragement.

180. Mistakes help me learn.

181. I am making mistakes, but I am improving.

182. I am pushing myself.

183. I am able to adjust.

184. I will keep moving forward.

185. I am facing obstacles, not stoppers.

186. I am an overcomer.

187. I am an achiever. 188. I am worthy of the good things in my life.

189. I am not afraid of tomorrow.

190. I am getting better every day.

191. I am facing my problems.

192. I am accepting of setbacks, but I will not let them stop me.

193. I am dedicated to personal growth.

194. I am making positive change in my life.

195. I am open to learning new things.

196. I am ready to learn new things.

197. I am doing my best.

198. To be good at something, I must practice, practice, practice.

199. I am proud of who I am.

200. I am resilient and strong.

Try This! Create a "Resilience Jar." Write each of these affirmations on small pieces of paper and put them in a jar. Whenever you face a challenge or feel discouraged, pull out an affirmation from the jar. Read it aloud, think about what it means to you, and how you can apply it to your current situation. This jar can be your go-to source of encouragement when times get tough!

CHAPTER 5: AFFIRMATIONS FOR SELF-ESTEEM

You've probably heard that words can't hurt you. That's not always true; words can hurt - if you let them. We live in a world where people can be unkind to each other - sometimes on purpose and sometimes without meaning to. The best way to keep enjoying life is to have high self-esteem, to have enough confidence in yourself to know that the negative things you're being told aren't true. Frederick Douglass, an abolitionist and early civil rights leader, said it best: "The soul that is within me no man can degrade."

Here are some affirmations to help build your self-esteem:

201. I am responsible for me.

202. I am enthusiastic about life.

203. I am celebrating myself.

204. I am happy being me.

205. I am worthy of respect.

206. I am capable of sharing good ideas.

207. I am enjoying life.

208. I can find good in even tough situations.

209. My challenges prepare me for the future.

210. I am joyful.

211. I can do what I set my mind to doing.

212. I am worthy of respect.

213. I respect myself.

214. I am the only me in the whole wide world.

215. I am special.

216. I am important.

217. I am brave.

218. I am confident.

219. I feel good about the future.

220. I feel good about myself.

221. I have the right to be happy.

222. I encourage myself.

223. I am honest.

224. I am truthful.

225. I am in control of my thoughts

226. I am in control of my actions.

227. I am my own person.

228. I have a happy heart.

229. I am in control of my emotions.

230. I am in control of me, even when I feel scared.

231. Whatever I am feeling is valid for me.

232. I am choosing to have a good attitude.

233. I am relaxed even in stressful moments.

234. I am good looking.

235. I am in control of my attitude.

236. I am enterprising.

237. I am self-assured.

238. I am hard-working.

239. I determine my worth, not others.

240. I am making the most of opportunities that come my way.

241. I am actively seeking new opportunities.

242. I love all people.

243. I know there will be opportunities coming soon.

244. I am deserving of the good that comes my way.

245. I am attentive.

246. I am focused on the here and now.

247. I am looking forward to the future.

248. I am cherishing the past.

249. I am controlling what I can and rolling with the rest.

250. I am appreciative of all that I have.

251. I am replacing negative thoughts with realistic ones.

252. I am looking on the bright side while acknowledging the difficulties I face.

253. I am buoyant.

254. I am cheerful.

255. I am encouraging.

256. I am decisive.

257. I am sure in what I do.

258. I am a visionary.

259. I am unshakeable; I will succeed.

260. I am appreciative of other people.

261. I am seeking fulfillment and meaning in my life.

262. I am thankful for the skills and talents I have.

263. I am changing in a positive direction.

264. I am comfortable expressing my wants and needs.

265. I am living according to my values.

266. I am guided by principles.

267. I always give my very best.

268. I am setting my goals high, but realistic.

269. I can defend my ideas with logic.

270. I am using positive self-talk.

271. I push myself to do my best.

272. I set small goals to overcome my weaknesses.

273. I focus on building my strengths.

274. I adjust to setbacks if they happen.

275. I do not take rejection personally.

276. I am able to influence others to see my point of view.

277. I do not fear rejection.

278. I am holding myself accountable for what I say.

279. I am holding myself accountable for what I do.

280. If I am having feelings of guilt or fear, I am asking myself why and overcoming them.

281. I am willing to try new approaches.

282. I am adapting to new technologies.

283. I am accepting the past; I can't change it.

284. I am confident about the future; I can influence it.

285. I am influencing the future at this moment.

286. I am comfortable with change.

287. I am energetic.

288. I am owning up to my failings.

289. I am accepting blame if I deserve it.

290. I am taking responsibility for my actions.

291. I am transparent.

292. I am open.

293. I have pure motives for what I do.

294. I do not wish anybody harm.

295. I will succeed in life.

296. I am not scared of hard work.

297. I am sensitive to other people's feelings.

298. I am sensitive to other people's needs.

299. I energize myself with positive self-talk.

300. I am empowered.

CHAPTER 6:
AFFIRMATIONS FOR INNER PEACE/OVERCOMING STRESS

Stress is like gasoline; a little bit makes our engine go. If we don't have any stress, we aren't going to have any drive. However, if we have too much stress, we lose control. Having some stress actually brings satisfaction; just ask anyone who finds no purpose in life. As with most things in life, we don't want too little or too much; we need just the right amount.

Inner peace means finding calm within yourself no matter how crazy the world is around you. Inner peace means having found the right amount of stress, not too little and not too much. It means that you are content with both yourself and the world. As American singer and actress Janelle Monae said, "Even if it makes others uncomfortable, I will love who I am."

Here are some affirmations to help you find that peace:

301. I am at peace.

302. I am giving myself permission to relax.

303. I am calm in a crisis.

304. I am able to handle any challenge that comes my way.

305. Stress motivates me.

306. I am seeing beauty all around me.

307. I am in control of my life.

308. I am what I say and do.

309. I am finding new things about myself with each challenge I face.

310. I am at peace inside of myself even when things are stressful outside of me.

311. I am patient.

312. I am kind.

313. I am slow to anger.

314. I am ignoring people who want to tear me down.

315. I am glad to be me.

316. I am worthy of the care I give myself.

317. I am able to overcome my fears.

318. I am forgiving of those who hurt me.

319. I am planning, not worrying.

320. I love me -- and I love others too.

321. I love others -- and I love me too.

322. I am releasing my stress in positive ways.

323. I am collected.

324. I am not worrying about things over which I have no control.

325. I am poised.

326. I am steady.

327. I am unflustered.

328. I have a clear conscience.

329. I am composed.

330. I am chill.

331. I am pulling myself together.

332. I am relaxed when I go to bed.

333. I focus on the good things that happened to me as my day ends.

334. I look forward to a bright tomorrow.

335. I am gentle.

336. I am peaceful.

337. I find beauty in sunny days and in cloudy days.

338. I am laid-back.

339. I am well balanced.

340. I am easy-going.

341. I am unflappable.

342. I am mellow.

343. I am self-controlled.

344. I am addressing problems as they happen.

345. I am taking things in stride.

346. I am nipping problems in the bud.

347. I am planting seeds for my future.

348. I forgive myself for my mistakes.

349. I accept my faults and strive to overcome them.

350. I know life has its ups and downs, but I have the ability to influence it to have an upward trend.

351. I am savoring my achievements.

352. I am celebrating my successes.

353. I am focusing on the positive aspects of my life.

354. I am accepting when others disagree with me.

355. I have high expectations of myself, but realize I can't control others.

356. I try to do as much of a task as time allows.

357. I am working hard on "important matters", but everything that is urgent is not important.

358. I am learning from hardships.

359. I am moving beyond my hardships.

360. I am able to laugh at myself.

361. I use positive language around other people.

362. I am an encourager.

363. I don't stress over things that don't matter.

364. I am capable of keeping secrets.

365. I am someone others can always turn to.

366. I am a hard worker, but I also take time to relax.

367. I am doing what is right for me.

368. I am kind to myself, and I get the nutrition and exercise I need.

369. I don't take on more than I can handle.

370. I am comfortable telling people, "No."

371. I am living my life as I believe it should be lived.

372. I am walking away from toxic situations.

373. I am getting proper rest.

374. I am developing good habits.

375. I am following good routines.

376. I am reasonable in the amount of pressure I put on myself.

377. I am building a network of adults and peers who support me.

378. I am expanding my skillset.

379. I am accepting that life is unpredictable and my plans may need to be adjusted.

380. I am accepting that I cannot control everything.

381. I am in control of my emotions.

382. I am able to relax.

383. I am able to stay relaxed even in stressful environments.

384. I am willing to walk away if things get too tense.

385. I am planning my day.

386. I am showing myself compassion.

387. I focus on one thing at a time -- and do it well.

388. I am allowing myself enough time so I don't have to rush.

389. I am setting aside technology to enjoy people and nature.

390. I am spending time with friends and loved ones.

391. I give thanks for my blessings.

392. I am telling people thank-you when they do something for me.

393. I am appreciative.

394. I am willing to help others, even if they can't do anything for me.

395. I am making time to rejuvenate.

396. I can lighten a tense mood.

397. I am not repeating gossip.

398. I am comfortable asking people to respect my boundaries.

399. I am willing to respect other people's boundaries.

400. I know everything is going to work out fine.

CHAPTER 7: AFFIRMATIONS FOR LEADING

You are a leader. If you aren't yet, you will be. That's right, like it or not, you are going to be a leader. You may be the leader of your family, of a club, or at recess. Later in life, you will be the leader of your family, a community organization, your child's club, or your work. Leading is a big responsibility, but it should not be shunned. Leaders make a difference, and, as Michelle Obama said, there is "so much history yet to be made."

Here are some affirmations to help you develop your leadership skills:

401. I set a good example for others.

402. I can make choices when I need to.

403. I take care of myself.

404. I help others when they need it.

405. I take my jobs seriously.

406. I do what's right, even if it's not popular.

407. I try to understand how others feel.

408. I speak up for myself without being mean.

409. I stand up for what I believe is right.

410. I'm not afraid to share my ideas.

411. I am becoming a good leader.

412. I know it's okay if people don't always agree with me.

413. I try to fix problems when I see them.

414. I listen when someone gives me advice to improve.

415. I like getting feedback to help me do better.

416. If something goes wrong, I try to make it right.

417. I focus on what's important.

418. I help my friends learn new things too.

419. I always try my best on projects.

420. I'm brave enough to make tough choices.

421. I have the courage to do what's right.

422. I work on learning new skills.

423. I look for ways to grow and improve.

424. I care about how others feel.

425. I care about the people in my team or group.

426. I can ask others for help when I need it.

427. I trust my friends and classmates.

428. I am a good listener.

429. I like hearing good ideas from everyone.

430. I am okay with things changing.

431. I focus on getting things done.

432. I am willing to help my teammates.

433. I follow through on my plans.

434. I love learning new things.

435. I set a good example for others.

436. I'm open to ideas that aren't my own.

437. I finish what I start.

438. I come up with creative ideas.

439. I enjoy working with others.

440. I'm becoming a better leader every day.

441. I'm proud of my team or group.

442. I can find something good about everyone in my group.

443. I encourage others to do their best.

444. I think about what needs to be done ahead of time.

445. I believe we can do a good job on our project.

446. I encourage my team to do their very best.

447. I'm excited about what we're doing.

448. I get things done.

449. I'm good at helping others stay on task.

450. I'm ready to handle problems if they come up.

451. I am a good communicator.

452. I am humble.

453. I am proud of who I am.

454. I am proud of my team when we try our best, even if we aren't perfect.

455. I am always trying to improve myself.

456. I lead by setting a good example.

457. I keep my eye on our goal.

458. I give my teammates honest and kind feedback.

459. I can give compliments when they are deserved.

460. I can accept compliments graciously.

461. I respect everyone on my team.

462. I know what I'm good at and what I need to work on.

463. I respect other people's boundaries.

464. I take time to think about my actions.

465. I understand my own feelings and actions.

466. I am open and honest with others.

467. I can think of ways to solve problems.

468. I care about others' feelings.

469. I think ahead about what might happen.

470. I set reasonable deadlines and try to meet them.

471. I enjoy taking charge when it's my turn.

472. I can help calm arguments between group members.

473. I can explain our team's goals clearly.

474. I'm not afraid to ask for help when I need it.

475. I am always learning new things about being a leader.

476. I can bounce back from setbacks.

477. I stay positive even when things don't go as planned.

478. I help create a friendly team spirit.

479. I pay attention to small details too.

480. I set high but achievable goals for myself.

481. I encourage my team to do their best.

482. I can help guide others.

483. I inspire others to do good things.

484. I can adjust to new situations.

485. I come up with creative solutions to problems.

486. I give credit to others when they do well.

487. People can count on me.

488. I do what I say I'll do.

489. I show up on time.

490. I use my time wisely.

491. I'm committed to learning and growing.

492. I trust my instincts after I understand a problem.

493. I'm hopeful but realistic.

494. I look people in the eye when I talk to them.

495. I can see the big picture.

496. I'm not afraid to try new things.

497. I help others become leaders.

498. I can explain my ideas clearly.

499. I can back up what I say with facts.

500. I can adapt when things change.

CHAPTER 8: AFFIRMATIONS FOR SOCIAL INTERACTION

No matter who we are, we can't do everything by ourselves. We need other people. We're part of a community, and within that community, we must get along with others.

It can be tempting to be unkind or not do our share, especially if we see others doing those things. Dr. Martin Luther King, Jr., reminded us not to fall into those traps, saying, "The time is always right to do what is right." These affirmations will help you remember how to behave kindly in your relationships with others.

Here are some affirmations to help you with social interactions:

501. I am my true self.

502. I treat others the way I want to be treated.

503. I am kind to everyone, even if they're not kind to me.

504. I treat all people with respect.

505. I am proud of where I come from.

506. I don't return meanness with meanness.

507. I share with others.

508. I care for others.

509. I help those around me.

510. I contribute to my family in meaningful ways.

511. I try to do the right thing.

512. I don't pay attention to those who try to put me down.

513. I respect other people's boundaries.

514. I am a caring person.

515. I care about my family.

516. I care about my community.

517. I care about nature.

518. I have good manners.

519. I accept opinions that are different from mine.

520. I am friendly.

521. I am a person who shares.

522. I am a person who cares.

523. I listen to others, even if I don't agree.

524. I pay attention when others are talking.

525. I try to be friendly to everyone.

526. I like to make others smile.

527. I know it's okay for people to be different.

528. I try to find ways to solve problems with my friends.

529. I can find something nice about everyone.

530. I stay calm when I disagree with someone.

531. I use my words, not my hands, to solve problems.

532. I talk about my feelings with people I trust.

533. I help my friends when they're sad or upset.

534. I learn new things from my friends and family.

535. I work well with others in a group.

536. I let others be the leader sometimes.

537. I'm polite to everyone.

538. I know it's okay to say "no" nicely.

539. I try to understand how others feel.

540. I help my family when they need me.

541. I make my own choices, even if they're different from my friends.

542. I speak up for myself in a nice way.

543. I'm brave when I have to talk in front of others.

544. I share my ideas with others.

545. I use kind words when I talk.

546. I try to include everyone in games and activities.

547. I know I have people who care about me.

548. I can play different roles in a group.

549. I'm fun to be around.

550. I tell jokes that make people laugh, not feel bad.

551. I respect how other people feel.

552. I respect myself and others.

553. I help people who need it.

554. I'm a good friend to anyone who needs one.

555. I choose my friends wisely.

556. I hang out with people who believe in me.

557. I try to be a good example for others.

558. I'm a good influence on my friends.

559. I lead by doing the right thing.

560. I work well with other people.

561. I'm good at getting along with others.

562. I support my friends and classmates.

563. I'm friendly and easy to talk to.

564. I believe in myself and others.

565. I do what I say I'll do.

566. I try to understand others.

567. I spend time with friends who help me be my best self.

568. I'm happy when good things happen to my friends.

569. I am myself around others.

570. I think about others' feelings.

571. I keep my promises.

572. I accept people for who they are.

573. I set a good example for others.

574. I control my actions.

575. I'm open to new ideas.

576. I show my friends I care about them.

577. I'm willing to help out when needed.

578. I try to understand how others feel.

579. I'm brave in social situations.

580. I believe in myself when I'm with others.

581. I can control my emotions around others.

582. I contribute to my group or team.

583. I'm happy to work with anyone, no matter who they are.

584. I look for ways to make things better.

585. I think before I speak or act.

586. I can make a difference in my community.

587. I stand up for what's right.

588. I'm not afraid to ask questions.

589. I respect others' opinions.

590. I learn from people who are different from me.

591. I am hanging out with people who help me stay on a wholesome path.

592. I am happy when other people have success.

593. I am affectionate.

594. I am thoughtful.

595. I am consistent.

596. I am tolerant.

597. I am capable of making a difference in the world.

598. I'm kind to everyone, even if they're different from me

599. I am always looking for ways to make life better.

600. I am accountable to myself as well as to others.

CHAPTER 9: AFFIRMATIONS FOR POSITIVE ATTITUDE

Do you believe that these affirmations are going to work? If you said yes, they likely will. However, if you said no, they likely will not.

Those who expect them to work are going to put in the time and energy to make them work. Those who don't expect them to work are not going to put in the time and energy needed to make them work. Your attitude in this and most other things determines if you will be successful.

If you believe that you can be a success, you can be a success. On the other hand, if you believe that you can only be mediocre, you will likely be only mediocre. Having a positive attitude is not just "willing" something into existence, but it is motivating you to make the effort and give it the thought required to bring it about.

Booker T. Washington, the founder of Tuskegee University, declared, "Character is power." Are you a positive character? It's not always easy to be one, because everyone encounters setbacks, but with a positive attitude those setbacks are mere bumps along the highway of life. Here are some affirmations to set and keep a positive attitude:

601. I am an optimistic person.

602. I see opportunities in every problem.

603. I surround myself with great people.

604. I can handle this.

605. I am confident in my abilities.

606. I greet each day with a smile.

607. I am satisfied.

608. I am self-assured.

609. I enjoy life.

610. My skin color is beautiful.

611. I can work well by myself.

612. I can work well with other people

613. I have a great attitude.

614. I can make a difference.

615. I am at peace with the world.

616. I am thankful.

617. I count my blessings.

618. I am helping other people.

619. I am focusing on building my strengths.

620. I am overcoming my weaknesses.

621. I take time to laugh.

622. I take time to reflect.

623. I find time to relax.

624. I'm excited about what's coming next.

625. I am expressing myself in positive words

626. I know the future will be grand.

627. I make good plans for my day.

628. I believe the future will be great.

629. I use positive words when I talk.

630. I think of good things about myself.

631. I show my feelings in a healthy way.

632. I know it's okay to make mistakes while learning.

633. I ask for help to improve.

634. I'm on the way to a good life.

635. I am making good plans for my life.

636. I like trying new things.

637. I think about good things before I go to sleep.

638. I'm around people I look up to.

639. I choose how I feel, not what happens around me.

640. I can think of clever ways to solve problems.

641. I wear a smile on my face.

642. I look for the good in every situation.

643. I don't give up easily.

644. I finish what I start.

645. I see challenges as chances to learn.

646. I keep going even when things are tough.

647. I spend time with people who are positive.

648. I'm willing to grow and change.

649. I celebrate small wins on the way to big goals.

650. I have a kind heart.

651. I learn from both good and bad experiences.

652. I count my blessings every night.

653. I surround myself with good people.

654. I give true compliments to others.

655. I find the good in other people.

656. I enjoy encouraging others.

657. I take care of my body.

658. I take care of my mind.

659. I am a caring person.

660. I like being around others.

661. I take care of my feelings.

662. I make time to do things that are good for me.

663. I practice to get better at things.

664. I'm on the path to sucess.

665. I choose to forgive others.

666. I break big goals into smaller, easier steps.

667. I talk about my feelings instead of keeping them inside.

668. I have close friends I can trust.

669. I eat foods that are good for me.

670. I am sharpening my skills

671. I have a bedtime routine to help me sleep well.

672. I enjoy reading regularly.

673. I value what others think and feel.

674. I have special talents to share with others.

675. I picture myself reaching my goals.

676. I can think of new plans if my first plan doesn't work.

677. I use my time to do useful things.

678. I want to get things done.

679. I balance learning, playing, and resting.

680. I find something positive in each day.

681. I create my own happiness.

682. I look for solutions instead of complaining.

683. I am nice to everyone I meet.

684. I celebrate small victories on the way to the big prize

685. I take action instead of waiting around.

686. I take responsibility for what I say and do.

687. I get closer to my goals each day.

688. I use kind words when I talk.

689. I share my worries with someone I trust.

690. I know what's important to me.

691. I try to make others' lives better.

692. I stand up straight and hold my head high.

693. I keep trying, even when things are hard.

694. I remember nice things people have said about me.

695. I don't make big deals out of small problems.

696. I focus on things I can control.

697. I hope for the best, but I prepare for challenges.

698. I believe tomorrow will be a great day.

699. I feel good because I did my very best.

700. I believe challenges are an opportunity to gain experience.

CHAPTER 10: AFFIRMATIONS FOR MAKING THE WORLD A BETTER PLACE

You can make a big difference in the world, even at your age! When we help others, we're not only making their lives better, but we're also making ourselves feel good. It's like planting seeds of kindness that grow into a better world for everyone.

Author Toni Morrison said, "Make a difference about something other than yourselves." When you grow up, will your family and community be better because of you? I hope so! The difference you make might help one person or it could help your whole community. President Barack Obama encouraged us to think about our country, asking, "Do we care to make America as good as it can be?"

701. I am making things better for myself and others.

702. I am making a difference.

703. The future can be even better than today.

704. I am part of a group of people who want to help others.

705. I am deserving of being heard.

706. I am helping to make good changes in the world.

707. I am speaking up about things that matter.

708. I am helping to make my community better.

709. I look for better ways to do things.

710. I am someone who likes to give.

711. I think about others as well as myself.

712. I love my country and know we can always improve.

713. When I see a problem, I try to help fix it.

714. I care about my community.

715. I am a good neighbor.

716. I am brave when facing hard things.

717. I stay positive even when times are tough.

718. I'm ready for new challenges.

719. I encourage others to help our community too.

720. I face problems instead of ignoring them.

721. I think about others' needs, not just my own.

722. I like doing good things for people.

723. I share my time and things with others.

724. I care about other people's well-being.

725. I want to make my community better for everyone.

726. I am considerate.

727. I show concern for others.

728. I am never too young to make a difference.

729. I care about my community.

730. I have a big heart.

731. I stand up for things I believe in.

732. I am responsible in my community.

733. I care about the environment.

734. I am a citizen of the world.

735. I am active in my community.

736. I learn about different cultures.

737. I spread goodwill.

738. I am eager to help.

739. I take action to help.

740. I am making the world a better place.

741. I am aware of issues in my community and my world.

742. I am trying to learn more about the issues in my community and my world.

743. I ask "why" to understand things better.

744. I am not scared to speak up.

745. I am respectful toward the people I want to help.

746. I am respectful to people who don't agree with me.

747. I can explain why I feel the way I do about issues.

748. I try to help every day, not just during special times.

749. I am willing to stand up for what I believe in.

750. I'm okay with people disagreeing with me.

751. I am sure my actions will make a difference.

752. I am learning how our government works.

753. I stick to my values unless I learn a better way.

754. I am committed to what I believe in.

755. I know what I stand against.

756. I know what I stand for.

757. I can make someone else's day better.

758. I do the right thing in the right way.

759. I am who I am.

760. I help others in my own way.

761. I take care of my mind.

762. I listen to my heart when it comes to helping people.

763. I help others not just for a day, but for a long time.

764. I care about my surroundings.

765. I'm happy just helping, I don't need rewards.

766. I live by what I believe.

767. I can see that things aren't always simple.

768. I'm proud to be part of my community.

769. I won't let others treat me unfairly.

770. I help make the world better.

771. I show I care by being active in my community.

772. I include everyone.

773. I pay attention to what's happening around me.

774. I talk to others nicely, even if we disagree.

775. I show respect for people in charge.

776. I care about fairness.

777. I want to improve my community.

778. I'm willing to help make my community better.

779. I think about the good things I've done to help others.

780. I speak up for what I believe in, not what others tell me to say.

781. I am brave.

782. I look for ways I can make things better.

783. I'm not afraid to help others.

784. I teach others about things that are important to me.

785. I use my talents to do good.

786. I don't give up easily.

787. I inspire others.

788. I'm willing to work hard to make big changes.

789. I help in ways that feel right to me.

790. My energy can make good things happen.

791. I form my own opinions.

792. I do good things for my community.

793. I listen to and try to understand different ideas.

794. I'm learning to think carefully about things.

795. I care about the people around me.

796. I do some volunteer work.

797. I'm my own person, but I look up to people who help others.

798. I respect others who try to make the world better.

799. I pay attention to what's happening in the world.

800. I work hard because the world needs my help.

CHAPTER 11: AFFIRMATIONS FOR GRATITUDE

"Gratitude" is a big word that means being thankful and appreciating what we have. When we practice gratitude, we're noticing all the good things in our lives and saying "thank you" for them.

In a world where we often want more and more things, it's easy to forget to be thankful for what we already have. Being grateful helps us see how lucky we are. As poet Alice Walker said, "Thank you is the best prayer that anyone could say."

Remember, people won't always remember to thank you. Amy Jacques Garvey, an important African-American journalist, said, "Keep going, even if people don't always show they appreciate you." These affirmations will remind you to take time to appreciate what you have and the people around you.

801. I am grateful for the air I breathe.

802. I am thankful for my talents.

803. I am grateful to those who came before me.

804. I am taking time to count my blessings.

805. I am thankful to be living right now.

806. I am grateful to my teachers.

807. I focus on the good things I have, not what I don't have.

808. I count my blessings, no matter how small.

809. I am thankful for my freedom.

810. I am thankful for my friends.

811. I am thankful for those who help me learn.

812. I am thankful for my health.

813. I am thankful for my senses: seeing, hearing, tasting, smelling, and touching.

814. I encourage others and celebrate when they do well.

815. I accept myself as I am while also trying to be better.

816. I am thankful for my food.

817. I am thankful for what I have, knowing some people have less.

818. I am thankful for challenges, because they help me grow.

819. I am thankful for the chances I get.

820. I am thankful for my mind that can think.

821. I am thankful for people who disagree with me, because they help me think more.

822. I am thankful for those who teach me right from wrong.

823. I am thankful for my country.

824. I am thankful for the people who run our country, even if I don't always agree with them.

825. I am thankful for my home.

826. I focus on what I have, and don't worry about what I don't.

827. I'm happy when others do well, even if I didn't win.

828. I fill my mind with happy thoughts and things I'm thankful for.

829. I am thankful for my life experiences and the stories I can tell.

830. I am thankful for my connections to others.

831. I am thankful for problems, because they make me stronger.

832. I am thankful even in tough times, because I have many blessings.

833. The world doesn't owe me anything; everything I have is a gift.

834. I am thankful for rain, because it helps plants grow.

835. I am grateful I was created.

836. I am thankful for rainbows and when storms pass.

837. I am thankful for victories, no matter how small.

838. I enjoy every minute of life.

839. I am grateful for hope.

840. I can be happy, even during hard times.

841. I am thankful that I can choose to be happy.

842. I am thankful for happiness inside me, not from things I own.

843. I forgive those who hurt me.

844. I forgive those who don't meet my expectations.

845. I am grateful for this book.

846. I am grateful I can choose my attitude.

847. I am grateful I can make my own choices.

848. I am grateful for the ability to overcome hard times.

849. I do kind things to show people I appreciate them.

850. I am thankful for warm showers.

851. I take time each day to think about how good life is to me.

852. I say thank you to people who do nice things for me.

853. I give honest compliments to others.

854. At the end of each day, I think about what made me happy.

855. I am thankful for clean water to drink.

856. I am thankful for the people who keep me safe.

857. I am grateful for the ability to feel love.

858. I am grateful to everyone who helps take care of me.

859. I am thankful for sunshine.

860. I am thankful for plants and trees.

861. I am thankful for being able to talk and listen.

862. I am thankful for books and things that help me learn.

863. I stop to notice the beauty of nature around me.

864. I am thankful for my bed.

865. I am grateful I can see colors.

866. I am thankful for medicines and doctors.

867. I am thankful for pets and animals.

868. I am thankful for the advice I get.

869. I am thankful for my family.

870. I am grateful for a good night's sleep.

871. I am thankful for the lessons I learn when things go wrong.

872. I am thankful for each new day when I wake up.

873. I am thankful for blue skies and pretty nature.

874. I am thankful for beautiful sunsets.

875. I am grateful for chances to visit new places.

876. I am grateful for people who help me.

877. I am grateful for ways to talk to friends far away.

878. I am thankful for having a bathroom in my home.

879. I am thankful for technology that makes life easier.

880. I am thankful for new adventures.

881. I am thankful for school and the chance to learn.

882. I am thankful for being able to write.

883. I am thankful for my dreams and ideas.

884. I am thankful for my conscience that helps me know right from wrong.

885. I appreciate little things, like the air I breathe.

886. I am thankful for those who take time to help me.

887. I am thankful for the beauty of the earth.

888. I am thankful for good friends.

889. I am thankful for my talents.

890. I am thankful for being unique.

891. I am living a wonderful life.

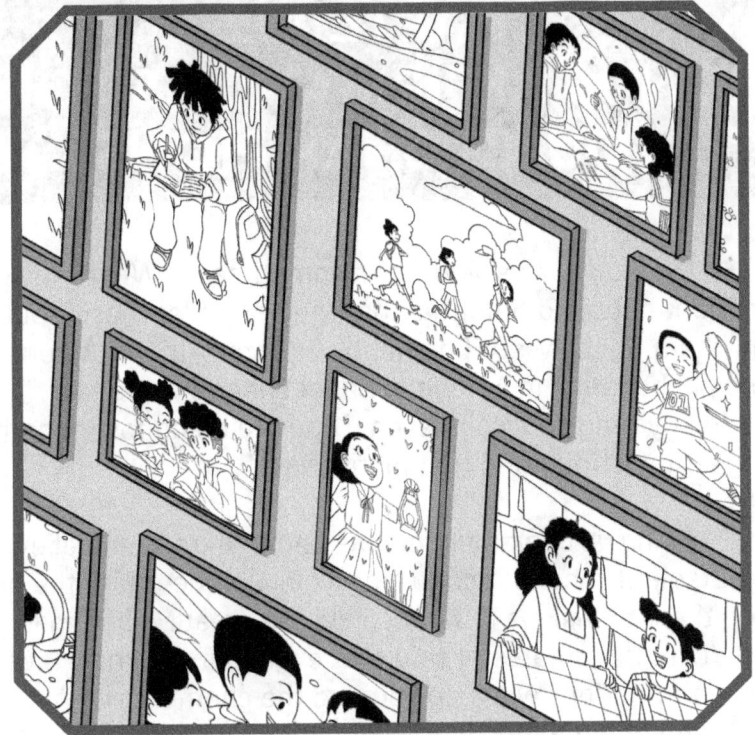

892. I am thankful for memories and photos of good times.

893. I cherish today.

894. I am thankful for things I usually take for granted, like being able to walk.

895. I am thankful for my health.

896. I am a thankful person.

897. I appreciate the helpful people in my life.

898. I am thankful for the food I have.

899. I am grateful for my amazing body.

900. I am thankful for another day of life.

CHAPTER 12:
BONUS AFFIRMATIONS FOR YOUNG CHAMPIONS

Everyone has doubts sometimes. What makes confident people different is that they don't let these doubts hold them back. Misty Copeland, the first African American principal ballerina in American Ballet Theatre, once said, "You can do anything you want, even if you are being told negative things. Stay strong and find motivation."

Being a champion means more than just believing in yourself. It means recognizing your unique strengths and using them to make a difference. As the great Muhammad Ali said, "I am the greatest. I said that even before I knew I was." These affirmations will help you find the champion within you and let that champion shine every day.

901. I am proud of my heritage and the color of my skin.

902. I am developing strong values rooted in my family's traditions.

903. I celebrate my unique features and personal style.

904. My efforts in school are building towards a bright future.

905. I embrace and learn from people of all backgrounds.

906. My curiosity about my history makes me a strong learner.

907. I balance my activities to become well-rounded and successful.

908. I appreciate art from my culture and around the world.

909. My actions can create positive change in my community.

910. My creativity and imagination know no bounds.

911. I find strength in the wisdom of my elders.

912. My ancestry is a source of pride and inspiration.

913. I use social media to connect positively with my community.

914. I express myself through art forms that speak to my soul.

915. Reading about the achievements of people like me inspires me.

916. I am proud of the music and stories from my culture.

917. I can be a champion for my neighborhood and the environment.

918. I celebrate the accomplishments of those who came before me.

919. I respect my own boundaries and those of others.

920. I face new experiences with the courage of my ancestors.

921. My words have the power to uplift and inspire others.

922. I pursue interests that reflect and celebrate who I am.

923. I enjoy activities that keep me strong and healthy.

924. My focus helps me overcome challenges, just like the leaders I admire.

925. I use technology to learn about and celebrate my heritage.

926. I carry the strength of generations within me.

927. My voice matters in every conversation.

928. I find beauty in the diversity of my community.

929. My dreams are valid and achievable.

930. I embrace the wisdom passed down through my family.

931. My natural hair is beautiful and versatile.

932. I am writing my own story of success.

933. I see role models who look like me in many fields.

934. My cultural traditions enrich my life.

935. I am resilient in the face of challenges.

936. My perspective is unique and valuable.

937. My skills in math and science can help improve my world.

938. My creativity knows no limits.

939. I am comfortable in my own skin.

940. I stand tall and proud of who I am.

941. My language and dialect are part of my identity.

942. I am creating a positive legacy for future generations.

943. I find strength in my community's unity.

944. My potential is limitless.

945. I honor my roots while growing towards my future.

946. I am worthy of respect and fair treatment.

947. My experiences shape my understanding of the world.

948. I contribute to the richness of my culture.

949. I am constantly learning and evolving.

950. My success inspires others in my community.

951. I am worthy of love, respect, and success.

952. My curiosity leads me to new discoveries every day.

953. I embrace challenges as opportunities to grow.

954. My imagination is a powerful tool for creating change.

955. I celebrate the unique qualities that make me who I am.

956. My voice carries weight and wisdom beyond my years.

957. I am building a future filled with possibility.

958. My empathy helps me understand and connect with others.

959. I have the courage to stand up for what's right.

960. My creativity finds expression in everything I do.

961. I am resilient in the face of setbacks.

962. My ideas have the power to inspire others.

963. I approach each day with enthusiasm and optimism.

964. My determination helps me overcome obstacles.

965. I am capable of overcoming any obstacle.

966. My actions today shape the person I'll become tomorrow.

967. I find strength in my family's stories and experiences.

968. My kindness creates ripples of positivity around me.

969. I embrace my emotions as a source of strength.

970. My dreams are valid and worth pursuing.

971. I contribute unique value to my community.

972. My perseverance turns challenges into achievements.

973. I approach new experiences with an open mind.

974. My self-respect guides my decisions and actions.

975. I am capable of creating positive change in the world.

976. I am confident in my abilities and potential.

977. My thoughts and ideas are worthy of being heard.

978. I embrace my natural talents and work to develop them.

979. My integrity shines through in all my actions.

980. I am resilient and can bounce back from any setback.

981. My uniqueness is my strength in this diverse world.

982. I approach learning with excitement and curiosity.

983. My self-care is important and deserves attention.

984. I cultivate peace within myself and spread it to others.

985. My goals are achievable with persistence and hard work.

986. I am developing leadership skills every day.

987. My compassion makes the world a better place.

988. I embrace change as an opportunity for growth.

989. My words have the power to uplift and encourage.

990. I am building a strong foundation for my future.

991. My patience allows me to persevere through challenges.

992. I approach problems with creativity and innovation.

993. I am the author of my own story.

994. My authenticity is valued and appreciated.

995. My positive attitude influences those around me.

996. I am capable of achieving greatness in my own unique way.

997. My courage allows me to face fears and overcome them.

998. I embrace my journey of self-discovery and growth.

999. My presence adds value to every situation.

1000. I am constantly evolving into the best version of myself.

PART 3
WRITING AFFIRMATIONS

CHAPTER 13: CREATE YOUR OWN POWERFUL AFFIRMATIONS!

Hey there, affirmation superstar! You've learned about lots of amazing affirmations in this book, but what if you want to create your very own? That's what this chapter is all about – making affirmations that are 100% you!

YOUR AFFIRMATION TOOLKIT

Creating your own affirmations is like being a chef in the kitchen of your mind. You've got all these awesome ingredients (that's you and your experiences!), and now it's time to cook up something special. Here are two super cool ways to whip up your own affirmations:

METHOD 1: START WITH WHAT MAKES YOU AWESOME

1. Think about something that makes you great. Maybe it's your kindness, your smarts, or how proud you are of your beautiful brown skin.

2. Start with "I am..." Remember, we're talking about the awesome you right now!

3. Add your greatness. For example: "I am kind" or "I am proud of my heritage."

4. Make it pop! Try "I am a beacon of kindness in my community" or "I am a proud carrier of my ancestors' strength."
Your turn! What makes you awesome?

I am _____

METHOD 2:
REMIX AN INSPIRING QUOTE

1. Think of a cool quote from a Black hero you admire. Like when Issa Rae said, "I'm rooting for everybody Black."

2. Take the main idea. Issa's quote is about supporting and celebrating Black excellence.

3. Turn it into your own "I am" statement. For example: "I am a supporter of Black excellence."

4. Make it personal: "I am a champion for my Black peers and community."

Now you try! Got a favorite quote? Turn it into your affirmation:

I am _____

- Tips for Crafting Super-Charged Affirmations
- Keep it positive! "I am confident" beats "I am not shy."
- Make it now, not later. "I am" is your power phrase!
- Short and sweet wins the race. Think tweet, not essay.
- Use words that make you feel like a superhero.
- One power per affirmation – you've got plenty of time to make more!
- Make it true to your experiences as a young Black person.

Stuck? Try the Flip-It Technique!

If you're drawing a blank, here's a cool trick:

1. Write down something that's bugging you. Example: "I'm nervous about my dance recital."

2. Ask why. "Because I think I might mess up."

3. Flip it around. "I perform my dance routines with confidence."

4. Make it an affirmation: "I am a confident dancer who shines on stage!"

Your turn! Try the Flip-It Technique:

1. What's bugging you? _____

2. Why? _____

3. Flip it: _____

4. Your affirmation: I am _____

Your Affirmation Challenge

Now that you're an affirmation-creating pro, here's your challenge: Create three affirmations that celebrate different parts of who you are. Maybe one about your mind, one about your body, and one about your spirit or culture. Go for it!

1. I am _____

2. I am _____

3. I am _____

Amazing job! Remember, your affirmations are like your personal power-up phrases. Use them every day to remind yourself just how incredible you are. You've got this!

CONCLUSION

Alright, affirmation superstar! Don't worry if you're not a pro at writing affirmations yet. It's like learning to ride a bike - it takes practice, but you'll get there!

In this chapter, we've learned:

1. How to build an awesome affirmation
2. Cool tips to make your affirmations super powerful
3. Tricks to help when you're stuck

Now, here's a secret: You're not just writing affirmations - you're becoming your own personal coach! Just like a basketball or dance coach helps their team get ready for the big game or recital, you're getting yourself ready for whatever comes your way.
Think about it:

- At night, you can think about what you want to rock tomorrow.
- At the end of each day, you can think about what went great and what you want to do even better next time.

Being your own coach isn't always easy, but guess what? You've got an amazing student - YOU! There will be days when you feel like you've won the championship, and days when things don't go as planned. But with your affirmations as your secret weapon, you'll be able to handle anything that comes your way.

Remember, you are strong, you are smart, and you are capable of amazing things. Keep practicing those affirmations, and watch yourself shine brighter every day!

Now, for one last challenge: Write an affirmation that celebrates how awesome you are as your own coach. Start with "I am..."

I am _____

Way to go, coach! You're on your way to being an affirmation champion!

www.ingramcontent.com/pod-product-compliance
Lightning Source LLC
Chambersburg PA
CBHW071103120626
46546CB00003B/1257